Finding God Next to Me

Exercises to Restore the Soul

Rodney A Drury

Redneck Mystic Media
3011 N. Delaware Street
Peoria IL 61603

Scripture quotations taken from the New American Standard Bible® (NASB), Copyright © 1960, 1962, 1963, 1968, 1971, 1972, 1973, 1975, 1977, 1995 by The Lockman Foundation Used by permission. www.Lockman.org

Contents

Here is the code breaker. It is also in the back of this book

A	⬡	N	ïi
B	ïǀ	O	◇
C	◇	P	◇⊶
D	⚲	Q	⫼·
E	⬚	R	◇⬚
F	◇	S	♀
G	⚲	T	⚲
h	8	U	‖
i	ǀ☐	V	∞
j	⊖	W	·ᵢ̇
k	☐ǃ	X	ꓕ
l	·8	Y	·ᴛ
m	⊖⊖	z	ᴛ

Introduction

I wrote this book for myself. Because I often forget what I have learned along the way, I believe that this book is one way for me to remember what I have forgotten about my life with God. I have over 50 journals I need to unpack in some way. This is my first attempt at this.

I also want my kids and grandkids to see what it is like to live a life of more creativity and less production... Have -more time to be with God and less time on our own. I also want to resolve the Mary/Martha debate of John 11 with a "YES, I am actively waiting on God."

And I want to help people, who like me, may have a hard time not thinking and people who love God and get burdened by their own thoughts, emotions, and desires... People who need a dose of perspective each day... People who want to integrate categories of science, politics, religion, art, love, faith, hope, truth, justice, and hard work.

This is my first attempt, so I set my expectation of getting a "C". Maybe a high "C". And maybe as you work your way through this book, you can find that you too enjoy being average, normal, common. For it is with the common, everyday person with whom Christ Jesus walks.

If you are extraordinary, you most likely don't need this book. But if you are wonderful (full of wonder), this book might help you enjoy your life more by increasing your awareness of God's triune presence.

Friendship with God

Read the Gospel of John one chapter at a time. After each chapter, ponder on what it would be like to be a friend of Jesus. Here are some questions to use if you need them.

- What is God telling you about Himself through the story? What's the big picture?
- What are the likes and dislikes of God?
- Are there certain kinds of people Jesus connects to better than others? Why is John called the beloved and the others are not?
- What kind of people keep having conflicts with God?

As you become more and more a friend of God look for….

- How God uses time.
    - Time to be with people
    - Time to meet needs
    - Time to do the will of God and the work of the Kingdom of God
- When is Jesus easy to be around?
- When is it more difficult to be around Jesus?

Branding

Definition: The marketing practice of creating a name, symbol or design that identifies and differentiates a product from other products.

from https://www.entrepreneur.com

Many of us bought into branding as part of our culture and we didn't even question it. For example, water now comes in plastic bottles, so I don't need to transport it in my canteen any more. Great! It's not that I think about having water in a bottle V.S. a jug, it is just that way.

But since branding seeks to identify and differentiate us (the product of Christianity), it actually moves eyes and ears away from God and onto the created. So, we end up seeking to be special, unique, different, or important. Maybe we even seek to be such a good product that we try to become perfect.

The result is that we end up comparing ourselves to others and trying to hide all our faults and failures. I love the Bible because it exposes all my faults and failures. The Bible is the story of God and mankind which shows that people are full of problems and God is full of solutions.

Look at all the stuff we do to stand out, to be seen, to be valued, loved and significant. Look at what the Christian churches do to blend into our culture, and How do we market ourselves.

I am for marketing. That term was called witnessing in the first century church. "Witness" became a prototype or word that came to signify martyr. So do I want to be a unique prototype or a martyr?

Many people say that the foundation of your brand is your logo. Look at all the logos in the church world today. Now ponder the two early logos of the people of God.   They were the Cross and the Fish (ichthys).

Make some Logos for your life. Draw out your ideas here. How can we help people see that it is God, not people that is the essence of Christianity? Also, how can we communicate to modern man without destroying the historical Jesus?

Desire for God

Desire for help, or to be loved
Desire for hope, or for healing

Longing for purpose
Concern to be good

Reading His record
Pondering His creation

Tired of being alone

Afraid of being afraid

Enjoying a sunrise

Resting in bed

Who taught me to fear

Not the one who put two trees in the garden

Not the one who made me by hand

Not the one who has no fear himself

Not the one who calls me to sacrifice all so that I have

Not the one who provides endless life

Not the one who says over and over again "fear not"

It was not my Father in heaven who taught me to fear.

◇◇◇◇◇◇ ◇◇◇◇

Psalm 9

A full heart sings.
Half-hearted complains.

ꝗ8◈ⅰⅰ☐!♀

Remembering the good give life.
Pondering pain, despairing.

Who are you? Does your name tell me? Can I trust you, your name?
◇ꝗ☐–⊖☖!☐◈◇ꝗ

God is a friend that protects. He is powerful in His presence.

A cry for justice is a cry for God and A longing for someone to know, understand, love, care and defend.

☖ ⊖⊖☖♀ꝗ 8!☐◻8

Who can care for us all? Who is able to rule the world with truth and righteousness?

Evil is like the night; it's time will end. A day is coming where there will be only light. Temporary powers will run into the end. Beginning a new day.

◇ꝗ◈◇ꝗ

Do not despair that you fight for good, justice and truth. You fight not alone, you fight not forever. A day has been set, a time established for all evil to end. Freedom.

If you remove the Lord God, you remove all hope for the poor and oppressed. Mankind does not care for its kind.

Those who truly seek the Lord find Him. Though the mountain be high, all effort is rewarded. Though days are long, all struggle is satisfied. Great treasure has great cost.

⬭⬨⬩ ⎮◻♀ ⬭⬨⬩

The song of my life reflects all things in His hands. I do not fear because I know the one who rules fear. Even while I work, endure, my soul sings.

God cares for the killer. He loves those who love not.

Divine justice is more than consequences for actions. It is redemption; it is forgiveness; it is new life; new hope. Yet some do not like such justice.

⬩◊⬨◊⬡⬭⎮◻♀♀⬭ⁱⁱ⬭♀♀

I am rejected, disliked, belittled, abandoned, betrayed, thought stupid, overlooked, and ignored. Yet none of this pollutes my soul or transforms my identity.

A perfect God has grace for my imperfections. I am a man and He does not judge me as though I was a god.

There is one who will always help.

⟜⊖⬭◊⬡⬭◊ˈ⊤

I have fallen into the pit I have dug. I have conceived my own destruction and now, here I lie. And here is God next to me.

It helps little to think of how good I am or how bad I am if at the same time I do not think more of God.

◊⊗◊╤▢♀ ⯑◊◊◊╤ ⯑8▢ ◊⊶◊◊◊╤

God does not just judge people, but nations, races, ethnic groups.

May I be a blessing to my people, the race that gave me life, the nation that sustains me.

⊖‖♀⯑

The needy and the poor are always on the mind of God. When He comes He often comes first to them. May I be with them when He comes.

When I cannot give money to the poor and needy, may I freely give love.

▢‖▢ii⯑

No man will prevail. No good, or great or godly. No man.

When I fully embrace my humanity, then I can invite God's divinity into my soul and walk in harmony with both God and man.

Unlike the people of the past, I see my leader as n*either* God nor the answer, but a servant. Good or bad, just or unjust, pleasing on unpleasing I know how they live is crying out to me. **"Live best for each life touches another."**

Complaining prayer is just as effective as trying to direct the wind.

Reading the word of God and not hearing it is like feasting on a warm bowl of water.

I will build a great life upon a million tiny choices of simple goodness.

⌐⌐⊖'T ⋕8⊒ ⵕ⋕⊒⊖⵵⋕⊘⊖ⵕ⋕ ·8⋩♥♥⊒ ⋩⵵⟡ ⋕8⊒ ·8⋩⟡⵵⊖
⌐⌐⋩ⵕⵕ 8|▢◁8⵵ ⵵⟡|▢·8·8 'T⋩‼ ⁔·|▢⵵8 ⵔ⊒·8|▢◁8⵵, ⌐⋩'T
⊖ⵥⵔ ⟡⵵⊒⌐⋩|▢⵵|▢ⵥ▢|

Victorious Living

What is the overcoming life all about?

What is the key to being a Christian?

How do you live a happy, successful life in God?

What is the key to all things – practically?

1. Overcome fear
2. Surrender outcomes
3. Manifest joy, rejoice, and give thanks

This is what Father, Son and Holy Spirit are doing in our daily lives. This is how we are discipled by God. This is how we ….

Then Jesus said to His disciples, "If anyone wishes to come after Me, he must deny himself, and take up his cross and follow Me. "For whoever wishes to save his life will lose it; but whoever loses his life for My sake will find it. "For what will it profit a man if he gains the whole world and forfeits his soul? Or what will a man give in exchange for his soul?

Matthew 16:24-26

A Day of Small Thinking

To forgive, detach the thing that is controlling your soul and give control again to God

Forgiveness exists because there is some of God in all of us.

Whenever I think, "I don't need to be forgiven," I most assuredly do.

If you make people earn forgiveness, you can no longer give it.

The time it takes to forgive is the time it takes to bring your pain to God and hope again.

Some things need to be forgiven, some ignored.

It is normal to be treated poorly by others; the wonder is in being loved.

Conflict doesn't mean you don't have value, only that values clash.

Rejection, abandonment, and betrayal are fertilizer for the soul.

We are often blamed for not accomplishing someone else's dreams for them.

"I want," has officially replaced, "I should."

We say "no' to the wrong things by saying "yes" to the right things. Learn to say "yes" to the best things and fill your life with them.

People turn to totalitarian rulers after they have allowed society to rule for a while.

Self-control determines how just you are.

Passion does not justify actions any more than war justifies truth.

A Society that is against slavery does not promote drug use.

WE promote Hopelessness by proclaiming helplessness and Fear by declaring ourselves a victim.

One does not need to change the world in order to be significant, but only change ourselves.

The ability to endure pain gives courage to face lift.

You do not deserve a better life, for life is not offered in degrees of merit.

IF there were no God, people would treat you 100 times worse than they do now. People, not God, are evil.

Improvement takes more than self-help. It takes outside intervention.

"Not addicted" is not something we say, but do.

If you are hopeless, you are listening to the wrong voices.

It's OK to have a pity party as long as you know it doesn't help.

Master fears and set others free.

Discipline restores the soul. Laziness destroys your worth.

Being significant only requires that we do something of value for others.

Societies' most valued people help others.

Being teachable is a sign of healthy self-love.

If you can pray, you can change the world.

Prayer rooms are just as effective as platforms.

When I leave because I am dissatisfied, I have left my opportunity to make a difference.

Coveting one leader while following a different one is just making plans to abandon your spiritual family.

You are mature when someone of a lower rank can correct you. You are deceived when no one can.

The easy way is worthless.

Demanding that I be loved in a certain way or be treated in a certain way is like using my Xbox to control the weather.

Trying to make people happy, is impossible. They alone have that power.

We can give. We cannot make people receive.

Today I will seek healing for my past, and plant good seeds for my future.

John 11:35   Jesus wept.

Jehovah
Everlasting life
Savior
Uncreated
Suffering Servant
Weeping
Empathy
Pain
Tears

⟐⟐⟐⟐⟐⟐⟐⟐⟐ ⟐⟐⟐ ⟐⟐⟐⟐⟐, ⟐⟐⟐⟐⟐ ⟐⟐⟐⟐

Holy Spirit

Ponder why the Bible and God chose to use these images for the Holy Spirit.

Wind

Fire

Water

Dove

Tongues

The Example of Jesus

John 13:15 reads: "For I gave you an example that you also should do as I did to you.

---

the greatest among us who we call

Lord

and Master

the all wise leader,

Teacher, king

washed the feet, the heart, the soul

your heart prepared for where your

feet must go

How does God Guide Me?

Through His word

Impressions in prayer

Interruptions

Through lack and need

Eruptions of compassion

Counsel of friends and family

Rebukes, correction

Roadblocks and circumstances

Dreams and visions

Worry not, the Lord's skill in leading is greater than my ability to stay lost. All I need is a humble heart and willing spirit.

Enlightenment

How should I tell the world that I know the truth? Should I boast of dreams, visions, revelations? Should I promote myself or hide myself?

Light is not to be hidden nor shoved in someone's face. It is not my gifts that testify to the world: but my character.

We need gifted people of character.

> If I speak with the tongues of men and of angels, but do not have love, I have become a noisy gong or a clanging cymbal. If I have the gift of prophecy, and know all mysteries and all knowledge; and if I have all faith, so as to remove mountains, but do not have love, I am nothing. And if I give all my possessions to feed the poor, and if I surrender my body to be burned, but do not have love, it profits me nothing.
>
> 1 Corinthians 13:1-3

The enlightened promote both as one. They say to themselves and then others, grow in grace and gifts. Be great, in serving and in being silent. Make Christ known in all you do and in doing nothing.

IF

Pondering on 1 Corinthians 13:1-3

What does "if" mean?
A question
A condition
A request "if I could"
A condition

Learn the lesson of "if." It often tells us what we can have and the conditions for obtaining more.

⚲◈❑❂◈❑Ⅰ, ◈❂◈❑⚴◈❂8❑◈ᐟT, ❂❂⚴❑❑ ❂❂⚴‖ᣠ❂❑ᣠ⚲, ⋮◈❑❑8 ❓8❑ ◈❂⚴⚴◈ Ⅰ❑ᣠ ⋅8⚴❑❑

Burning with God

The angel of the LORD appeared to him in a blazing fire
from the midst of a bush; and he looked, and behold,
the bush was burning with fire, yet the bush was not
consumed.

Exodus 3:2

Did the bush become more than a bush when God came within? Did the bush stay the same, so that wonder might be known? Does God's fire make us special or is our normal divinely used? Is the bush the attraction or is the bush simply used?

How far will you press your own desires?

Read 1 Chronicles 20-21

20:1 David, had he not fought enough? Was he not deserving of a timer of rest while others fought?

20:4-8 Surely God was with David. Look at the victories. Should not David say in his heart that "I am the Lord's man?"

Is David wrong for seeing his life favored by the Lord?

David had favor, title, position. Was he to be prohibited from doing what his heart desired? Does he not give us such things for us to use as we desire?

21:3 A trusted proven friend counsels otherwise. But should I listen if it is not in my own heart?

Is it true that the only way out of deception is to trust someone else more than you trust yourself?

21:4 The king's word prevailed. A boss gets his/her way. A parent's will is accomplished. A pastor drives forward his plan.

Do we see the obedience, and the compliance of others as a sign of God's approval? If we get our way, surely it is God who made it so.

21:7 God was displeased and struck not the man, but the people. How is this just? Was it because kings know how kingdoms work? Is it because long ago men and women desired a man as king and rejected God?

21:11 The king who forced his desire still gets to choose still. What was God saying as he let David choose the fate of the people . Was it justice alone or a lesson too?

21:7 Humility is a great thing to desire. It bows easily in repentance. It is low enough to see the angle of the Lord. Humility prepares great men for worship.

21:22 What we once conquered, driven by desire and presumption, we now purchase at full price to establish a place of worship.

May you find within yourself a place of worship. A place where you paid the full price to have. A place in you that is given to Him.

21:30 Fear of the Lord is a good thing. It checks the heart of rulers and kings. It puts parents and pastors in their places. All under His rule and reign. All must be under His wisdom and ways.

Have my desires ever driven me to force my way on others?

Do I see my titles, positions, gifts, talents, or authority as a tool blessed by God?

Am I now, and will I always be, a tool in the hands of God?

Envy

I find that the people of God sometime use envy as a basic motivation for spiritual maturity. This is another way we take the eternal word of God and modernize it. By....

Incorrectly using "what God has done for others He will do for you."

Promoting one successful person as the role model for us all.

Promoting the elite, or the best and calling it normal, average.

By constantly comparing what one person does to another for the purpose of growth.

May these scriptures and quotes lead me past modern and into the eternal.

⌨ͥ∞'T

Envy is the art of counting the other fellow's blessings instead of your own. -Harold Coffin

Therefore, putting aside all malice and all deceit and hypocrisy and envy and all slander, like newborn babies, long for the pure milk of the word, so that by it you may grow in respect to salvation, if you have tasted the kindness of the Lord. 1 Peter 2:1-3 NASV

The envious person grows lean with the fatness of their neighbor. – Socrates

If anyone advocates a different doctrine and does not agree with sound words, those of our Lord Jesus Christ, and with the doctrine conforming to godliness, he is conceited and understands nothing; but he has a morbid interest in controversial questions and disputes about words, out of which arise envy, strife, abusive language, evil suspicions, and constant friction between men of depraved mind and deprived of the truth, who suppose that godliness is a means of gain. 1 Timothy 6:3-5 NASV

Oh, what a bitter thing it is to look into happiness through another man's eyes. -William Shakespeare

This wisdom is not that which comes down from above, but is earthly, natural, demonic. For where jealousy and selfish ambition exist, there is disorder and every evil thing. But the wisdom from above is first pure, then peaceable, gentle, reasonable, full of mercy and good fruits, unwavering, without hypocrisy. And the seed whose fruit is righteousness is sown in peace by those who make peace. James 3:15-18

Envy shoots at others and wounds itself. -English Proverb

"Whenever you attempt a good work you will find other men doing the same kind of work, and probably doing it better. Envy them not." -Henry Drummond

Now the deeds of the flesh are evident, which are: immorality, impurity, sensuality, idolatry, sorcery, enmities, strife, jealousy, outbursts of anger, disputes, dissensions, factions, envying, drunkenness, carousing, and things like these, of which I forewarn you, just as I have forewarned you, that those who practice such things will not inherit the kingdom of God. Galatians 5:19-21 NASV

"The cure for the sin of envy and jealousy is to find our contentment in God." - Jerry Bridge

"How many covet that they may boast? How many desire more glory for their flesh?" - Watchman Nee

How can I just see the other person and not see them through my issues?

How often am I offended just because someone does things different from me, but I want to control them and make them do it like me?

How often do I judge myself by others and overlook what God is saying and doing in me?

Words of Envy word search

```
M M Y E U N K M K Z D F Y C X
A Y A H V C P Y J I U R W O J
P T G L N A M M S E L Q K V X
R P C Q I S R C E A R P P E M
A E A O P C O C V S E R B T X
Z S T I V N E I A G S P E G N
Q E T F T E R W D E E R G Y S
B E S E A X T K K X N G D D I
B Y N S Y T K O M J T C U U O
C T N Y R X S P U L M M R X R
H X B H G T R U I S E C G R R
I K C O I I P L L W N U E N B
Y D E S I R E V U P T E B T G
S S E N R E T T I B W G S G R
H I C I E M V V V F L N F S T
```

BEGRUDGE	BITTERNESS	COVET
COVETOUSNESS	CRAVE	DESIRE
DISCONTENT	GREED	LUSTAFTER
MALICE	RESENTMENT	RIVALRY
SPITE		

Human Rights

Do humans have any rights?
I think the whole idea of human rights is an attempt to follow the teachings of Jesus, but without Him. Love, honor, care, forgiveness, justice; these are things of the kingdom of God, not evolved animals.

It seems we want to move beyond survival of the fittest but do not want to give up the foundation that premise is based on. We want to avoid being created by God but live as God intended. God's intention of justice, kindness, truth, and love are in the heart of humanity. These continue to witness about Him.

Grace

Related to human rights.

Some, sadly, now insist on grace. But grace demanded and required is far from God's grace. Undeserving is the condition for grace to exist. Even though Jesus died for me, and because Jesus died for me, I have a provision of grace.

How sad to take a gift given and say it was deserved. Why are we like that? Why do we even need to deserve? In what way is Jesus shamed by our being undeserving? In what we are? Are we faulted by our present condition of seeing grace as given, not earned or deserved?

Let us boast in the Lord, not in being favored.

Bonhoeffer Quotes

"Cheap grace is the preaching of forgiveness without requiring repentance, baptism without church discipline, Communion without confession, absolution without personal confession. Cheap grace is grace without discipleship, grace without the cross, grace without Jesus Christ."

- Dietrich Bonhoeffer

"Human love has little regard for the truth. It makes the truth relative, since nothing, not even the truth, must come between it and the beloved person."

- Dietrich Bonhoeffer

"One's task is not to turn the world upside down, but to do what is necessary at the given place and with a due consideration of reality."

- Dietrich Bonhoeffer

"God's truth judges created things out of love, and Satan's truth judges them out of envy and hatred."

- Dietrich Bonhoeffer

"God has reserved to Himself the right to determine the end of life, because He alone knows the goal to which it is His will to lead it. It is for Him alone to justify a life or to cast it away."

- Dietrich Bonhoeffer

"A Christian is someone who shares the sufferings of God in the world."

- Dietrich Bonhoeffer

"It is very easy to overestimate the importance of our own achievements in comparison with what we owe others."

- Dietrich Bonhoeffer

God Is....

Fill in the list

God is not controlling.

1. He will not force people who hate him to enter into His kingdom
2.
3.
4.
5.

God is not a whimp.

1. He endures rejection.
2.
3.
4.
5.

God is loving.

1. He is moved by pain and suffering.
2.
3.
4.
5.

God is full of joy.

1. God gives joy for our strength
2.
3.
4.
5.

I love....

Feeling good

Significance, being accepted

Having purpose, value, worth

Having respect, honor

My family, friends

My Job: helping others;

Leading; being in charge

Why do I love these things?

Are there things I don't love that I should?

Fear Not

In what area of my life am I failing to Fear Not?

Where am I calling fear faith?

How am I justifying fear as caution, wisdom, or insight?

TOP FEARS (internal and external)

1.

2.

3.

4.

5.

6.

7.

8.

Psalms 23

Read the Psalm and highlight the worlds that I feel God is highlighting. Ask myself "why is God speaking through this image/word? Is God desiring the image to speak to me as well as the words?

1 A Psalm of David. The LORD is my shepherd, I shall not want.

2 He makes me lie down in green pastures; He leads me beside quiet waters.

3 He restores my soul; He guides me in the paths of righteousness For His name's sake.

4 Even though I walk through the valley of the shadow of death, I fear no evil, for You are with me; Your rod and Your staff, they comfort me.

5 You prepare a table before me in the presence of my enemies; You have anointed my head with oil; My cup overflows.

6 Surely goodness and lovingkindness will follow me all the days of my life, And I will dwell in the house of the LORD forever.

Psalm 23 Highlighted Words to Ponder

Conversation with Jesus

Read John chapter 19
Now write out a conversation with Jesus as He hangs on the cross. Use your imagination to see Him there, to feel the breeze. Look on the faces of His mother and John. Look at the soldiers who are there?

Gaze on Jesus.

What do you see in His face?

Look at His body.

Ask for grace to see into His heart, what do you find there?

What would you ask Him?

What would you tell Him?

What emotions are strongest and why?

Conversation with Jesus note page.

꙰8꙰T ꙮ8◈·8·8 ·8꙰꙰◻! ◭ᵢᵢ 8!◻◶◶ ▬·8꙰◶◶ ꙰8꙰T
◇◦!◻꙰◇◦◇꙰8

Maze

How is life in God like a maze?

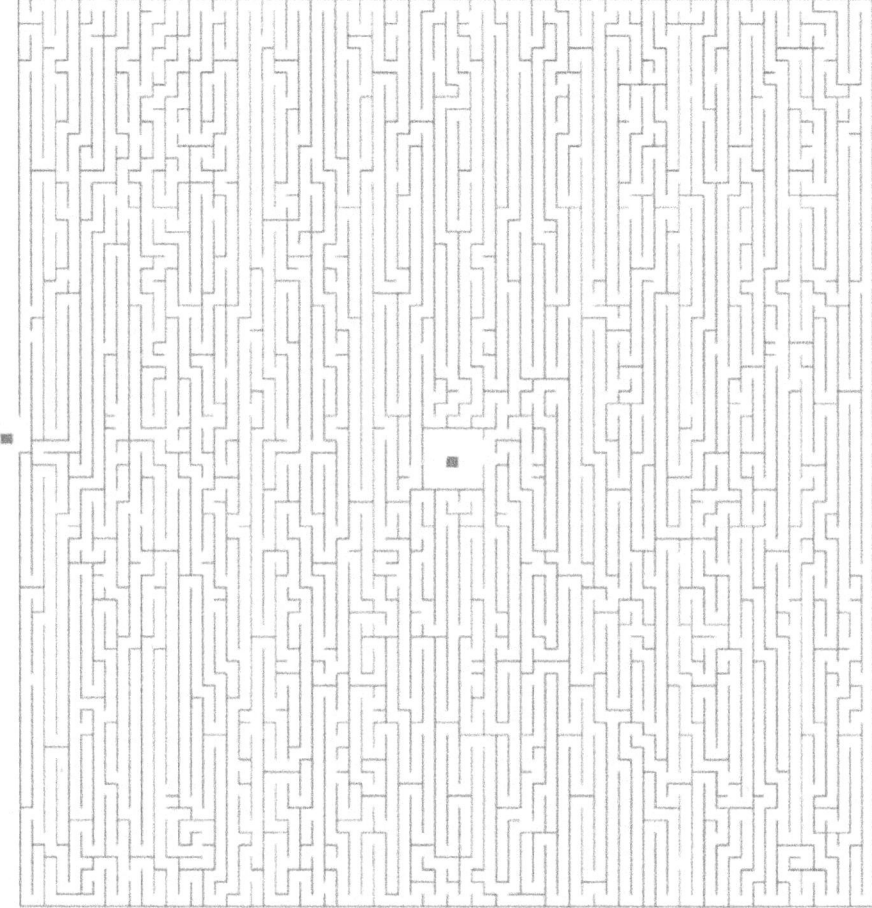

Alphabet God

Using the letter as a prompt, list something I like about God.

A

B

C

D

E

F

G

H

I

J

K

L

M

N

O

P

Q

R

S

T

U

V

W

X

Y

Z

Sowing and Reaping

Sowing and reaping is good when I am in pursuit of good things. But when I am in the place of reaping, what I have negatively sown, I want intervention, mercy, or someone to rescue me.

How can I be more aware of sowing and reaping in my life?

How can I not long for unjust intervention?

Often, I act one way around people, but that way I act is not the way I feel. I have reasons, excuses really, for my actions. I don't want to hurt them, I don't want to be confrontational, I don't want them to know what I really think.

That last one is the biggest. I want people to treat me like I want to be treated without telling them what I feel or think.

Hubris. Pride masquerading as meekness. A desire to control without the cost of confronting.

Am I expecting God to treat me favorably when I am failing to tell Him what I desire, long for and need?

Am I living a false life by not simply and lovely telling others what I desire, want or hope for in our relationships and behavior?

List of Partial Truths

Who gets on the list

Those I am only 25% honest with.

Those I am 50% honest with

Those I am 75 % honest with

Altered

I have a right to be understood
You must get me
You must comprehend my pain
My joy

But I don't get you
Why are you so strange
So unlike me
So independent of my ways

I fear that knowing you will burden me
Cause me to invest
Require I learn and listen
Why don't you change so I don't have to

The Trumpet Sound

When the three companies blew the trumpets and broke the pitchers, they held the torches in their left hands and the trumpets in their right hands for blowing, and cried, "A sword for the LORD and for Gideon!" Each stood in his place around the camp; and all the army ran, crying out as they fled.
Judges 7:20-21

When my sinful ways are attacked by the Light (torch) and Word (Trumpet) of God, I run.

The sin in me flees from the presence of the Lord and often carries with it my body, soul, and mind. I tend to run rather than submit while hoping for some way to come close to God and yet remain un-surrendered to the light and word.

And what do I cry out as I run?
"No one loves me."
"My life is so hard."
"This isn't my fault."
"But look what they are doing."

Surround me God so that in my running away I run into you.

How to be demonized

BE ANGRY, AND yet DO NOT SIN; do not let the sun go down on your anger, and do not give the devil an opportunity.
Ephesians 4:26-27

Slumber and anger = demonic opportunity.

- Resting in anger is not resting in the Lord.
- Passively enduring aggressive thoughts and actions results in open spiritual doors.
- Allowing myself to be angry is accomplished by the ongoing justification of anger and not avoiding dealing with it.
- Pride says, "you are right; just wait and they will see."

In Captivity

'For I know the plans that I have for you,' declares the LORD, 'plans for welfare and not for calamity to give you a future and a hope.
Jeremiah 29:11

This verse was given to those God was holding captive by Babylon for seventy years. Their welfare, peace, future, and hope were all a part of their captivity.

Freedom through confinement.
Independence through dependence.
Security through captivity.

This is one of the most popular verses in America. So how is God fulfilling this verse in your life? How is your long-term captivity and forced relocation working welfare, peace, a future, and hope in your life?

Parable of the Talents
Read Matthew 5:14-30

What are the possessions that God entrust to us?

God gives responsibility according to ability. Why?

Why isn't every one of the same equality?

What is the difference between ability and being loved? Do we only love the best? If we do, why?

"Good and faithful" was the verbal praise. Is that a praise we honor in our hearts?

Is there a relationship between fear and limited ability?

Does fear rob us of our rewards?

Why would someone battling fear also be battling wickedness and laziness?

Not properly taking care of the Lord's possessions according to our ability ends in a reward of removal. How does this show a just God speaking to the different motivations people have?

Church Leadership

Since day one, literally the first page of the Bible, the spiritual leader has been challenged.

If you only prepare to teach, minister, and serve, you are not preparing yourself enough. Prepare your heart and mind to be challenged.

Greed is everywhere.

People will want more and more from you, the church, and leadership. Learn to allow Father God to lead you and follow Him, not the demands of the people.

Responsibility and freedom.

Many people today live in lawlessness and call it freedom. The see and say responsibility is "religious" and they don't mean to care for widows and orphans.

Meditating on the law will help you see how love has boundaries.

Boasting, bragging, platforms, and positions.

A fool can be the king and a slave the wisest among us. Honor is not for the position you have but for the God who dwells in us all. If you introduce yourself as a prophet or apostle, you're probably not. Contrary to some teaching, you are not what you say you are.

Discernment of Spirits

Two of the most common tool used for discernment are anger and unforgiveness.

When we have anger, regardless of whether we know it or not, it clouds true spiritual insight. Anger tells us we have a right to judge which is very different than discernment. Anger locks the Holy Spirit in another room while it rants and raves its desires.

Unforgiveness causes our own sins not to be forgiven and we end up being crushed by our own sin and shame. Like a person being tortured, we yell and scream for justice. Yet we are torturing ourselves.

While justifying our inability to forgive we perform another grievous act upon our body and soul. With every thought of our right not to forgive we twist the soul in a knot of sorrow.

Remove the splinter from your eye.

Get help if you need to.

Black Hole Christians

Some Christians have avoided discipleship so long they have become black holes by sucking the life and light out of everything around them; they exist as a self-destructing swirl of self-centeredness.

Show great love to every black hole you meet. They are receiving in themselves enough pain and suffering. You do not need to add to it.

You most likely minister from afar. Minister through prayers. Minister by giving gifts and encouragement, not in person but through cards, notes, and media.

But any ministry will draw them near to find new light and life to feast upon. You do not need to fear this, only know that it will happen and have a plan with God for when it does.

And when you give to black holes, and do give but don't let them take, do not expect your gift to come back to you from men? Instead, look to God as your rewarder.

And do not be surprised if you receive much criticism and rejection for loving a black hole. Many have the mindset that if they are not able to do something, no one should be doing it for them.

But keep moving. Literally, when ministering around and to black holes, keep moving.

"Should I" fear

Should I live today in fear of what

> Might happen tomorrow?

Isn't that good planning, prudent?

> Unless it doesn't happen.

> Unless I miss joy today.

> Unless God has some better way for me.

They say, "Worry means you suffer twice."

> They say it because it is true, in part.

> But truly you suffer every day, all your life.

> Carrying an extra load of pain.

Day dream of joy, of hope, of love

> Fill your mind with things above

> Consider honor, beauty, wonder and awe.

It is not naive to do so.

> But wise, fruitful, and healthy.

> Empowering and holy.

"If you dressed for Friday's weather on Monday, what would you call yourself?"

Planning has actions to take that bring resolve; worry has no way to stop, to end, to resolve an action.

Box

This box often helps me think...

About God, about relationships, about the Holy Spirit.

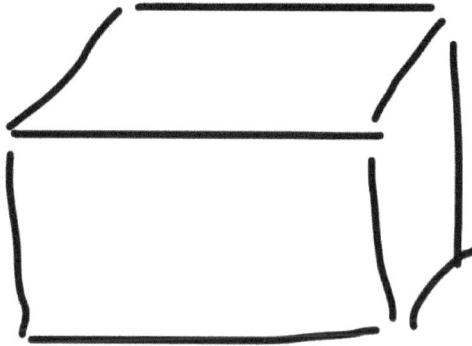

How is "in" different than "on"?

"With" different than "under"?

"Full" compared to "upon"?

Sometimes look at a box can help you understand life and God.

Help

John 14:26 "But the Helper, the Holy Spirit,

God is our helper. The Holy Spirit helps. We are called to help others. Helping is part of what we receive and do. Pondering "helping" helps us to see how God is working in our lives and how God uses us to help others.

Ways God …..

Makes easier

Resources

Serves

Assists

Supports

Aids

Guides

Comforts

Informs

Benefits

89

Ways God uses me to....

Makes easier

Resources

Serves

Assists

Supports

Aids

Guides

Comforts

Informs

Benefits

God helps my mind by....

And God uses my mind to help others by....

God helps my soul by....

God uses my soul to help others by....

God helps my body by....

God uses my body to help others by....

Use the box to help ponder 1

Passage with "help" from Psalms

Psa_5:2; Psa_12:1; Psa_18:6; Psa_18:41; Psa_20:2; Psa_22:11; Psa_22:19;
Psa_22:24; Psa_27:9; Psa_28:2; Psa_30:2; Psa_33:20; Psa_35:2;
Psa_38:22; Psa_40:13; Psa_40:17; Psa_42:5; Psa_42:11; Psa_43:5;
Psa_44:26; Psa_46:1; Psa_46:5; Psa_59:4; Psa_60:11; Psa_63:7; Psa_70:1;
Psa_70:5; Psa_71:12; Psa_72:12; Psa_79:9; Psa_83:8; Psa_88:13;
Psa_89:19; Psa_94:17; Psa_102:1; Psa_107:12; Psa_108:12; Psa_109:26;
Psa_115:9; Psa_115:10; Psa_115:11; Psa_118:7; Psa_119:86; Psa_119:147;
Psa_119:173; Psa_119:175; Psa_121:1; Psa_121:2; Psa_124:8; Psa_146:5.

Round for a reason

Each person is a gospel message
Good news to all, who Christ is
And like each Gospel
Unique
A varied expression, perspective
Not a different truth
A revelation of the light
With no shadow

Life, ministry, movement, history
Each with different allusion
Perspective of His light
Illustrated by the churches in Revelations
Seen in the gospels themselves
We experience God
As we live
As He lives in us
Illuminating

God And

Your voice, your heart, your life
>You are a Priest to God and for others
>You receive and give
>You love God and others
>>In the way you were made
>>Within God's will and ways

Stand, Standing, Upright

We should not seek approval as much as correction, acceptance as much as wisdom. Alone, we will one day stand before the Lord. Alone, we stand before Him now. But that alone empowers community. It establishes the one foundation on which we stand.

Vison for your life

Who gets the vision for your life?

Is it given to you through prophet, priest, or king?

Do you need to listen to others?

Are you all knowing?

Is uncertainty your sure foundation?

Who can tell you what to do?

Can you rule you own soul?

Some people struggle to see their life with meaning.

Some never desire significance. Some lazily say, "whatever."

You were created to be something and do something.

Your greatness is not determined by what you do, but how you do it with the being you are.

We can succeed by being better than someone and helping someone be better than we are.

Our life can be full by obtaining or by giving away.

Vision is not just the ability to see, but the ability to see others, to see God and to see how all is connected.

Thank God

Thanks, God, for hands to dig the soil
Thanks, God, for legs to share the load.
Thanks, God, for eyes to see the stranger.
Thanks, God, for hearts to welcome them home.
-     Ngatiawa River Monastery

Make a list of 15 simple everyday tasks or duties. Now write your everyday Thanks God verse?

Images

The images in the story of God are images that surround our lives each day. By taking the time to reflect on them we can see God in our story.

First think about what some images mean in the Bible.

Tree	Sun	Light
River	Water	grass
Sky	Shade	Day

Now use the pictures here or your surroundings and see what images of God's work are a part of your life today.

Images 2

What images do you have in your life and mind that reveals these words?

Love

Joy

Peace

Hope

Fear

Worry

Hunger

Justice

Kindness

Anger

Sin

Holiness

Truth

Spirit

Faith

Life

Dreams

```
Q N V I T M S M L S Y H M Y F
Y L E F I L S D S O T S N C S
R O E B F A E E A U V Z I V P
C A J F N J N H R K W E S S I
R H P Y T I D T R D N R R H R
O V H W L D N E C A E P E P I
J W A O R S I F A I T H G S T
A E H E L A K Y G H I L N S Z
A W A H C O Y E Y G U Z A K U
M M D O X Y T Y F R Q N U O N
S S Z X R S T R H G R E G L F
H A J Q R V A Y H X I O P E R
O S Z L D V M Q N X V F W M R
P G E J U S T I C E H A J A F
E Y X Q D D R K Q N H V B O M
```

ANGER	DREAMS	FAITH
FEAR	HOLINESS	HOPE
HUNGER	JOY	JUSTICE
KINDNESS	LIFE	LOVE
PEACE	SIN	SPIRIT
TRUTH	WORRY	

Values

What values do we have as American Christians?
What do we look for to see if someone is a successful Christian?

Here are my thoughts to get you thinking; make your own list.

Platform
Apostle, prophet, healing,
Popular, recognized
Influential, praised
Followers, rank in comparison to others
Intelligence,
Modern, culturally current

Now ponder what Jesus was looking for and desiring to develop as His disciples. Just look at these first followers and see what values God desired for them.

◈─☺─▯◇◁▯◇◈ii ◇‼·8◈‼◇◁▯ I▯♀ ii◬◔ ♀‼◇◇▯♀♀◁◇‼·8 I▯ii ◇8◇◁I▯♀◁▯◈ii▯◔T

Real Life

You have limits. "You can do all things through Christ Jesus" is a call to live your life, not to try to live out a fantasy life. Faith is not vain thinking. It is not a denial of reality. Faith in the presence and power of God in my reality.

Here are some circumstances that God wants to fill in your life, not remove. God wants to be with you where you are. Most of the time he leads us through, like His people leaving Egypt for the promise land.

Fill your circumstances with God and you will find God has filled your life with more then you need.

Limits that I invite God into with me

      Circumstances

      Seasons

      Talents/abilities

      Relationships

Ponder the context of "I can do all things."

Read the book of Philippians to see how a Godly man faces rejection, death, fear, hardships, pain, and suffering.

But I rejoiced in the Lord greatly, that now at last you have revived your concern for me; indeed, you were concerned before, but you lacked opportunity. Not that I speak from want, for I have learned to be content in whatever circumstances I am. I know how to get along with humble means, and I also know how to live in prosperity; in any and every circumstance I have learned the secret of being filled and going hungry, both of having abundance and suffering need. I can do all things through Him who strengthens me. Nevertheless, you have done well to share with me in my affliction.

Philippians 4:10-14

Do I spend more time worrying or rejoicing? In anxiety or in thanksgiving? Why?

Leadership and others

Two extremes to consider leadership by.

1) You are nothing without me.

2) I am nothing without you.

Christ Jesus and the Holy Spirit keep leading us into the reality that we and others are all something; we are never nothing.

So how do we turn away from choosing who to devalue?

How do we love others as ourselves as Jesus instructed?

How to love others as yourself in five words. Here is my list. Make one, too.

1. Honor
2. Kindness
3. Listen
4. Value
5. Courage

Productive or Creative

Some would say we do not need to choose between being productive or creative. However, having both is the best choice. And that might be true.

But many of us have lots to do and no creation in it. Maybe we create a social media post. Maybe we post a picture of a meal we made, an event we hosted, or an image of something we produced.

But take your Bible, your journal, your body and go to a place and try to think a thought you have never thought before.

Try to see the clouds, the sun, the rain in a way you never imagined.

Read a Psalm and imagine the setting, the field, the weather, the pain. Try to hear the voice, the sound, the way the words emerge from the lips.

Put your hand on your heart and make a meeting place for you and God in your heart. See his presence in you. See yourself loving Him, holding Him, speaking to Him.

Now make up a word, create a worn unknown, and unheard of before that describes your time with God.

Mine is in the code below

Eternal Life

1. I want it now

I find many people of God are not demanding eternal life now. They have been influenced by the powers of this world and claim their right, their entitlement to all that waits in eternity – now.

How do we balance living in the real world today and living in eternal life with Jesus?

How does Satan tempt us to live out of step with the Lord?

2. Justice

Many people will not have justice in this life. Eternity is the "time" and place for them. People, who in this life could never find justice will find endless justice in eternity.

Do I include eternity in my world view, or do I only live for this world?

Do I over value this temporary life and devalue eternal life?

3. A Ticket or a Transition
Do I gain eternal life because I bought a ticket called Salvation? Or is eternal life the continuation of my life now with God?

If I stop walking with God in this life, do I really want to walk with Him for all eternity? Would it be just for God to make me stay with Him if I didn't even like Him?

Now for this very reason also, applying all diligence, in your faith supply moral excellence, and in your moral excellence, knowledge, and in your knowledge, self-control, and in your self-control, perseverance, and in your perseverance, godliness, and in your godliness, brotherly kindness, and in your brotherly kindness, love. For if these qualities are yours and are increasing, they render you neither useless nor unfruitful in the true knowledge of our Lord Jesus Christ. For he who lacks these qualities is blind or short-sighted, having forgotten his purification from his former sins. Therefore, brethren, be all the more diligent to make certain about His calling and choosing you; for as long as you practice these things, you will never stumble; for in this way the entrance into the eternal kingdom of our Lord and Savior Jesus Christ will be abundantly supplied to you.

2 Peter 1:5-11

4. Righteousness and Justice lead to eternity

I was a stranger, and you did not invite Me in; naked, and you did not clothe Me; sick, and in prison, and you did not visit Me.' "Then they themselves also will answer, 'Lord, when did we see You hungry, or thirsty, or a stranger, or naked, or sick, or in prison, and did not take care of You?' "Then He will answer them, 'Truly I say to you, to the extent that you did not do it to one of the least of these, you did not do it to Me.' "These will go away into eternal punishment, but the righteous into eternal life."

Matthew 25:43-46

Does the Bible teach that "believing," as in what you think, is the key to life with God?

Does God judge the churches in Revelation according to their "deeds"?

The Two Great Commands, while involving what we think, focus on what we do. Have we allowed a division to come between what we think with what we do? When God makes us whole are we united in word and deed?

5. Eternal in the Gospels

Some emphasize this life. Others emphasize eternity. Listen to the Gospels and let the Holy Spirit lead you into the truth.

Here is a list of passages where the eternal appears in the Gospels. I wanted to see just what Jesus taught. I wanted to hear His words more than my own thoughts.

Each teaching does not stand along, but integrates with all the words of the Lord. So How can we have a big picture of eternity while still having particular teachings and insights?

Mat_18:8 "If your hand or your foot causes you to stumble, cut it off and throw it from you; it is better for you to enter life crippled or lame, than to have two hands or two feet and be cast into the eternal fire.

Mat_19:16 And someone came to Him and said, "Teacher, what good thing shall I do that I may obtain eternal life?"

Mat_19:29 "And everyone who has left houses or brothers or sisters or father or mother or children or farms for My name's sake, will receive many times as much, and will inherit eternal life.

Mat_25:41 "Then He will also say to those on His left, 'Depart from Me, accursed ones, into the eternal fire which has been prepared for the devil and his angels;

Mat_25:46 "These will go away into eternal punishment, but the righteous into eternal life."

Mar_3:29 but whoever blasphemes against the Holy Spirit never has forgiveness, but is guilty of an eternal sin"—

Mar_10:17 As He was setting out on a journey, a man ran up to Him and knelt before Him, and asked Him, "Good Teacher, what shall I do to inherit eternal life?"

Mar_10:30 But that he will receive a hundred times as much now in the present age, houses and brothers and sisters and mothers and children and farms, along with persecutions; and in the age to come, eternal life.

Mar_16:20 And they went out and preached everywhere, while the Lord worked with them, and confirmed the word by the signs that followed.] [And they promptly reported all these instructions to Peter and his companions. And after that, Jesus Himself sent out through them from east to west, the sacred and imperishable proclamation of eternal salvation.]

Luk_10:25 And a lawyer stood up and put Him to the test, saying, "Teacher, what shall I do to inherit eternal life?"

Luk_16:9 "And I say to you, make friends for yourselves by means of the wealth of unrighteousness, so that when it fails, they will receive you into the eternal dwellings.

Luk_18:18 A ruler questioned Him, saying, "Good Teacher, what shall I do to inherit eternal life?"

Luk_18:30 who will not receive many times as much at this time and in the age to come, eternal life."

Joh_3:15 so that whoever believes will in Him have eternal life.

Joh_3:16 "For God so loved the world, that He gave His only begotten Son, that whoever believes in Him shall not perish, but have eternal life.

Joh_3:36 "He who believes in the Son has eternal life; but he who does not obey the Son will not see life, but the wrath of God abides on him."

Joh_4:14 but whoever drinks of the water that I will give him shall never thirst; but the water that I will give him will become in him a well of water springing up to eternal life."

Joh_4:36 "Already he who reaps is receiving wages and is gathering fruit for life eternal; so that he who sows and he who reaps may rejoice together.

Joh_5:24 "Truly, truly, I say to you, he who hears My word, and believes Him who sent Me, has eternal life, and does not come into judgment, but has passed out of death into life.

Joh_5:39 "You search the Scriptures because you think that in them you have eternal life; it is these that testify about Me;

Joh_6:27 "Do not work for the food which perishes, but for the food which endures to eternal life, which the Son of Man will give to you, for on Him the Father, God, has set His seal."

Joh_6:40 "For this is the will of My Father, that everyone who beholds the Son and believes in Him will have eternal life, and I Myself will raise him up on the last day."

Joh_6:47 "Truly, truly, I say to you, he who believes has eternal life.

Joh_6:54 "He who eats My flesh and drinks My blood has eternal life, and I will raise him up on the last day.

Joh_6:68 Simon Peter answered Him, "Lord, to whom shall we go? You have words of eternal life.

Joh_10:28 and I give eternal life to them, and they will never perish; and no one will snatch them out of My hand.

Joh_12:25 "He who loves his life loses it, and he who hates his life in this world will keep it to life eternal.

Joh_12:50 "I know that His commandment is eternal life; therefore the things I speak, I speak just as the Father has told Me."

Joh_17:2 —even as You gave Him authority over all flesh, that to all whom You have given Him, He may give eternal life.

Joh_17:3 "This is eternal life, that they may know You, the only true God, and Jesus Christ whom You have sent.

Affliction

The natural man hates the fact that affliction and the invisible are so important. We often live by sight and the quest for happiness. And while sight and joy are great, they are not all that we live by or with.

> For momentary, light affliction is producing for us an eternal weight of glory far beyond all comparison, while we look not at the things which are seen, but at the things which are not seen; for the things which are seen are temporal, but the things which are not seen are eternal.
>
> 2 Corinthians 4:17-18

How does the pressure of this life strengthen me to endure the eternal weight of glory?

How do I overvalue this temporal life and under value the unseen?

My list of unseen things that I tend to overlook
Grace

Forgiveness

Fellowship with God

Life, unending

Significance forever

Spirit

Conviction

Truth

The true tabernacle

Heavens activity

Angles

Cloud of witnesses

Ministering Spirits

Ordinary Time

Half of the church year is called ordinary time. It means it is time ordered. It is not common or time with little or no purpose. But it is time we can order to be transformed by the Lord.

Time is one of the gifts God gives us.

I live better when I see each day as a gift. I live better because I value that day in a better way. I see that this day is not mine or about me. But this day is a gift for me, to me.

I might not be here tomorrow. Someone or many I love might be gone tonight. That should not produce fear but value. What I might call a distraction, I will call a delight if I see time as a gift to me, not a right I have.

Today I have been given the gift of time. I'm using that gift to read and write. I'll use that gift to eat meals and go to the gym. My gift will be spent on loving my wife and praying for my kids and grandkids.

I might use my gift to fret some about bills and grumble about the weather. I might allocate some of the gift to solving other people's problems.... Something no one asked me to do. But I'm sure once I get past a few moments of wasting my gift I will use it wisely again.

Thank you, Father, for the gift of time

Today I stand loved all day

I breath deep the joy of life

I see the wonders of creation

I hear laughter and joy, crying and pain

I did not earn this time

I cannot stop it

I cannot make it my own

I live a gifted life

A life in time

2Co 5:7 for we walk by faith, not by sight—

We move, adjust, shift

We advance, retreat, skip, stumble

We blunder, climb, ascend, fall

By trust, belief

By confidence

By pledge, alliance, loyalty

Not by vision or perception

Not by reason, logic, formulas

Not by a picture, display or Pinterest

The Light

The Way

The Life

Is not seen

But beheld

Not reasoned

But comprehended

Staring at a homeless man

I sat and stared at a homeless man

To see what I could see

Would it be evil or wretchedness

Would it be sin

Surely not peace

Can rotten teeth smile,

yes, they can

And a limp can skip

It's true

Sharing a cigarette instead of coin

Asking for help instead of praying to God

Facing rejection instead of deserving

Silently suffering instead of complaining

Can the unbathed be clean

Yes, they can

And a homeless heart can love

It is true

In Him is Life

I

Need

Help

In

Maturing

Inside

Spiritually

Loving

Inspiring

Free

Everyday

What is life?

Feeling	Decisions	Love
Aware	Breath	Time
Pain	Joy	Children
Friends	Work	Creativity
Rest	Learning	Adventure
Journey	Fellowship	Listening
Dark	Light	Seasons
Pressure	Rest	Gift

Bible Story Images

Have I ever been trapped doing God's will?

How did you I get free?

What tools did God provide?

Abraham and Lot had to part ways. How do I deal with family and following God?

Can I risk giving the other guy the first chance?

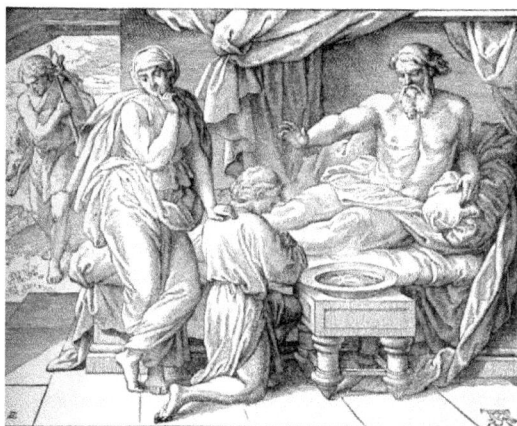

Jacob tricks Isaac. Do I use deception to better my life?

Do I use deception to serve God?

Jacob and Esau meet after the deception. What does deception do to family, to brotherhood?

What do I do when forgiven?

What was I doing when Jesus first called me?

What is the difference between believing in and following?

Following Jesus makes us into something. What am I being made into?

The greatest in the Kingdom of God is like a child.

How is a child of God a child?

Can I live under authority?

Ask your own questions

People to Pray For

Things to remember

The End

The end will come
Except it won't
For those in family with God

Strange thought
No end needed
For life in Him

No breaking of ties
No ending of love
No stopping at all

Hidden for a time
Requiring faith
Sure

But all good things take trust
All wonder involves
Imagination

When I'm gone
I won't be
Gone

My love for you
Will not just be a thought
It will be me- loving you

Code

Letter	Symbol	Letter	Symbol
A		N	
B		O	
C		P	
D		Q	
E		R	
F		S	
G		T	
h		U	
i		V	
j		W	
k		X	
l		Y	
m		z	

www.ingramcontent.com/pod-product-compliance
Lightning Source LLC
Chambersburg PA
CBHW081212020426

42331CB00012B/3003